BOLD, BLACK &
Beautiful Quilts

DEBBY KRATOVIL

Love to Quilt...

Located in Paducah, Kentucky, the American Quilter's Society (AQS) is dedicated to promoting the accomplishments of today's quilters. Through its publications and events, AQS strives to honor today's quiltmakers and their work and to inspire future creativity and innovation in quiltmaking.

EDITOR: TONI TOOMEY
GRAPHIC DESIGN: AMY CHASE
COVER DESIGN: MICHAEL BUCKINGHAM
QUILT PHOTOGRAPHY: CHARLES R. LYNCH
ILLUSTRATIONS: TONI TOOMEY AND DEBBY KRATOVIL

Library of Congress Cataloging-in-Publication Data

Kratovil, Debby.
  Bold, black & beautiful quilts / by Debby Kratovil.
      p. cm.
  ISBN 1-57432-857-3
  1. Patchwork--Patterns. 2. Quilting--Patterns. 3. Black in art. I. Title: Bold, black and beautiful quilts. II. Title

  TT835.K735 2004
  746.46'041--dc22

                              2004012379

Additional copies of this book may be ordered from the American Quilter's Society, PO Box 3290, Paducah, KY 42002-3290, or online at www.americanquilter.com.

Dedication

This book is dedicated to my long-suffering husband, Phil, who always allowed me to play with my fabric. He knew it would make me a happier wife and a kinder mother to our three beautiful daughters – Audrey, Hilary, and Valery.

Acknowledgments

I am eternally grateful to two special women. The first is my sister Janet Gawbill, who gave me my first computer when I was 40 years old. Little did she realize how it would dramatically change my life – introducing me to the world of writing, writing about quilting, and designing patterns and quilts. It was the missing link in my creativity. The second special woman is Jean Ann Wright, editor of *Quilt Magazine*. Ten years ago Jean asked if I could write about quilting and then bought my first story. She has been my biggest cheerleader and has always loved everything I write. I could not invent any more strategic people than these two women. My dream to write a book about quilting is realized today in large part due to them.

Table of Contents

Introduction

Today's quilters continue to be inspired by traditional designs. Time and again, no matter how far we travel in expressing our creative, artistic selves via the medium of quilts, we come back home to the established designs. Some of us are most comfortable making quilts based on favorite traditional patterns. Then some of us use the conventional patterns merely as a springboard for our creativity and thus create contemporary fiber art that pushes the envelope right to the edge.

While most of my quilts remain quite symmetrical, I have discovered that putting black in my quilts elevates them to a sensational and vivid level of visual experience. Black can add rich texture, create unusual settings, and stimulate the eye by presenting the unexpected. Black delivers a bold sensation that seems to heighten the feeling I want to communicate with each quilt. It is the icing on my fabric cake.

Let's face it. Some quilt patterns are not for the fainthearted. One look at them and we turn away and say, "Someday, but not today. Someday when I have the time. Someday when I have

nothing better to do than put together a thousand little tiny pieces all by hand." In our desire to create quilts, we find that time is the biggest enemy to completing our projects. Discovering quick ways to construct difficult or tedious blocks, settings, and borders frees us up to pursue, with confidence, those timeless, traditional designs that unite us to quilters of the past. In the process, we can enjoy our quilting more, happy to have more quilts to share with those we love. Therefore, I've included a quick appliqué method that bypasses the use of freezer paper and the need to turn under raw edges (page 46).

I hope that the quilt projects presented here will help you discover new tools for tackling your projects with confidence and that they will give you the foundation for creating new design possibilities.

Before You Begin

There are a few words of quilter's wisdom that I would like to share before you begin your first project in this book. As you may have already discovered, one element of a quilt can have different terms applied to it. In the section on the anatomy of a quilt I have defined some of the terms used in this book. Next, you will find some tips that make for smooth going for any quilting project – for any sewing project, for that matter. Finally, I give you my ten reasons for making a sample block before starting a project. It's the best advice I've ever given myself.

Anatomy of a Quilt

All quilts are composed of many different elements. Not all quilts contain the same elements, but rather have a mix of the items I describe here:

Appliqué block
A background piece of fabric with smaller pieces of fabric stitched onto it by hand or machine. These smaller fabric patches often have curved elements, such as flowers, leaves, or landscapes.

Alternate block
Either pieced, appliquéd, or plain fabric, this unit is positioned between your main blocks.

Backing
The fabric that covers the back of your quilt. It may be one large piece or several pieces sewn together.

Batting
The inside layer of a quilt that is sandwiched between the quilt top and its backing. Various fiber contents are available, including cotton, polyester, poly-cotton, wool, and silk.

Binding
A fabric strip stitched to and covering the outside raw edges of the quilt layers. It can be either a straight or a bias piece of fabric.

Border
One or more fabric frames around the main body of a quilt. Not all quilts have a border, while some have several of varying widths. Borders can be made from pieced units, fabric with appliqué designs, or just whole cloth.

Cornerstone
A square of plain fabric or composed of pieced fabrics which joins two adjacent sashing strips.

On Point
Any square block that is rotated 45 degrees so it stands on one corner. This block is usually set with four triangles to square it up again.

Pieced Block
Various shapes or patches of fabric stitched together into a larger unit. These form a design and can also be stitched by hand or machine.

Quilt Top
The upper part of a quilt layer that is composed of pieced blocks, appliqué blocks, a combination of the two, or a whole cloth. It can have sashings, borders, or any other variety of units.

Sashing Strip
Sometimes called a lattice strip, this is a fabric strip that separates blocks and rows of blocks.

Setting Triangle
Triangles (plain, pieced, or even appliquéd) added to square up the edges of blocks set on point.

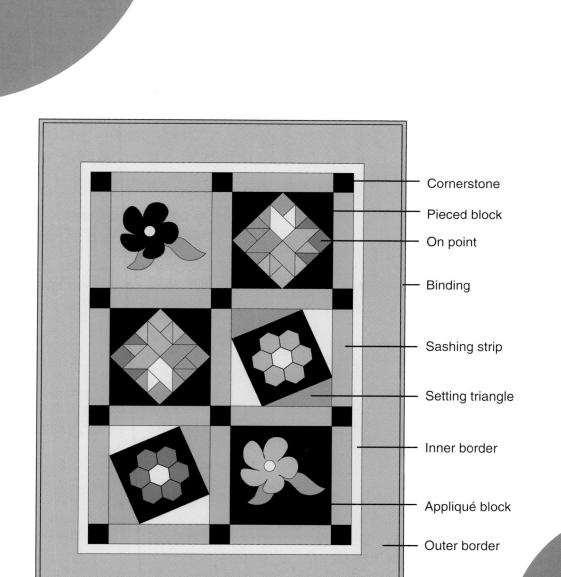

Cornerstone

Pieced block

On point

Binding

Sashing strip

Setting triangle

Inner border

Appliqué block

Outer border

Tips for Smooth Going

Keep your machine in working order

It is important to keep your sewing machine cleaned and oiled. (Warning: Certain electronic models DO NOT use any bobbin case lubrication. Be sure to read your owner's manual.) It is also helpful to check your machine's settings for each project. All sewing machines are not the same. Even the same machine will perform differently, depending on fabric content, fabric color, thread and batting choices.

Test your stitches

Practice your stitching using scraps of the same fabric as that in your project so that you can adjust your sewing machine settings. If you are going to use nylon monofilament for machine appliqué, make sure that the bobbin thread does not bleed up to the top of the block. This would require adjustments to your upper or lower tension settings.

Protect your ironing board

When working with fusible webbing, take care to protect your iron and ironing board with thin pieces of fabric or pressing sheets. Place one sheet under your work to keep any stray webbing from fusing to your ironing board. Then place another sheet over your work to keep stray webbing from sticking to your iron.

Look ahead at the directions

Before you begin cutting your fabric, read through all the directions at least once. Don't begin slicing and dicing without at least checking how you will cut the border fabrics. Sometimes the instructions require that you cut the border fabrics lengthwise first and then use the remainder of that fabric for some of the block patches.

Change your needle with each new project

Believe it or not, sewing machine needles grow weary after all that up and down exercise. Retire them before they do some serious damage. They get dull or even form a burr which can snag your fabric. It's a small price to pay for smooth sailing through your next project.

Respect for your rotary cutter

Take it from me, who lost a substantial section of my left index finger – pay attention when using that glorified pizza cutter. Keep your fingers close to the center of your acrylic ruler when using the rotary cutter with the other hand. Cut slowly – never toward you, always away from your body; change the blade at the first sign of skipping; get in the habit of snapping the blade shut after every cut. An open cutter is a dangerous weapon when dropped on your foot or accidentally scraped against a bare hand.

Ten Good Reasons for Sewing a Sample Block

Always cut and sew a sample block before cutting the entire quilt. Here are ten good reasons I have found for following my own advice!

1. Check template accuracy

There are times a printed template is incorrect in size. Just being off by ¼" will ruin the entire block. Just imagine if it were repeated 20, 30, or 40 times for an entire quilt. A sample block will show template accuracy or inaccuracy.

2. Check block size

The instructions may state that they are for a 12" block, but I have discovered more than once that my 12" block really sews up to be an 11" or 14" block! This is a good time to check the accuracy of the pattern, along with the ¼" seam allowance I think my sewing machine makes.

3. Test color and fabric choice

Sometimes it's hard to visualize how a block will look with my fabric choices until I actually sew it. I have rescued many a quilt by sewing a sample block with my first choice of fabric combinations, only to discover that those choices are not to my liking. I make a second sample block with new choices before I cut out the rest of the quilt.

4. Check number of pieces

On occasion, I have been so inspired by beautiful quilts made of intricately pieced blocks only to discover my enthusiasm wanes after making one or two blocks. One quilt I made had 24 blocks, and each block had 40 pieces, for a total of 960 pieces in that quilt. I was exhausted when I finished and vowed to always sew a sample block to help in my decision making.

5. Do I like the block?

Sometimes the colors are right, and there aren't too many pieces, but I don't like the result. Would I like it any better if I went on to make 20, 30, or even 40? Probably not. I quilt because I enjoy it, not just to acquire another bedcover.

6. Discover cutting shortcuts

Cutting out that first block starts my brain calculating ways to speed-cut the rest of the blocks. I see the way the template fits on the fabric strips, and I envision ways to not only cut out several of the same template at once but also how to conserve fabric in the process. If I'm going to cut out scores of blocks, I want to do it the quickest and easiest way possible.

7. Find sewing shortcuts

As I sew the first block, I think of ways to speed-sew sections of the block. Perhaps there are units within the block that I can sew all at once. Sewing and pressing similar units, assembly-line style, saves time.

8. Work out seam allowance direction

I find that most blocks require pressing the seam allowances to one side, but when the seams in one part of the block butt up against those in another part of the block, they fit more snugly when the allowances are pressed in opposite directions. Also, there are times when seam allowances need to be pressed open to eliminate bulk. Piecing that first block helps to work out these details.

9. Use a block to aid border selection

If I plan to make scores of the same block, but I haven't chosen my border and sashing fabric, it's quite easy to carry around one block to my favorite fabric stores to audition fabric for finishing my quilt.

10. Sample block provides inspiration

Having that first block hanging in front of me as I stitch the rest of them helps me see the sewing sequence and keep the pieces turned in the right direction as I sew. It generally inspires me to keep sewing, because I will soon have many more of the same block, in the same size, and in the same colors for a beautiful quilt.

GRANDMOTHER'S NIGHT GARDEN, 53" x 61", made by Debby Kratovil, Atlanta, Georgia. Machine quilted by Silvia Davis, Douglasville, Georgia.

Grandmother's Night Garden

Quilt size 49" x 61"
Block size 14" x 20"

A bright flower is bright even in the nighttime. I believe the flowers in my garden stay awake and tell stories to each other about all the things they saw and heard during the day. If we could see them against the backdrop of a dark night sky, we would see their colors glow in a special way. I tried to capture that in this rendition of my own garden.

Materials and Cutting Guide

(Use fabrics at least 42" wide. All strips are cut across the width unless stated otherwise.)

Materials	First Cut	Second Cut
template material	1 template from cutting pattern on page 14 1 template from seam line pattern on page 14	
black solid, 1⅛ yd	2 strips 14½" x 42" 5 strips 1" x 42" for inner border (pieced)	4 rectangles 14½" x 20½" for block backgrounds
bright yellow print, ¼ yd	1 strip 4½" x 42" 1 strip 2½" x 42" for checkerboard sashing	4 hexagon centers 1 sash 4½" x 18½"
bright green print, ½ yd	2 strips 4½" x 42" 2 strips 2½" x 42" for checkerboard sashing and four-patches	8 hexagon leaves 1 sash 4½" x 20½"
pink print, ⅞ yd	3 strips 4½" x 42" 2 strips 4½" x 42" for side borders (pieced with sashing remainders) 1 strip 2½" x 42" for checkerboard sashing	6 hexagon petals 1 sash 4½" x 20½" 1 sash 4½" x 22½"
blue print, ⅞ yd	2 strips 4½" x 42" 3 strips 4½" x 42" for top and bottom borders (pieced) 1 strip 2½" x 42" for checkerboard sashing	6 hexagon petals 1 sash 4½" x 20½"
orange print, ½ yd	2 strips 4½" x 42" 2 strips 2½" x 42" for checkerboard sashing and four-patches	6 hexagon petals 2 sashes 4½" x 18½"
purple print, ½ yd	2 strips 4½" x 42" 1 strip 2½" x 42" for checkerboard sashing	6 hexagon petals 1 sash 4½" x 20½"
bright multi-print on black background, ⅝ yd	6 strips 2½" x 42" for checkerboard sashing	
black and bright stripe, ½ yd	6 strips 2" x 42" for binding	
backing, 3½ yd	57" x 65" (pieced)	
batting	57" x 65"	

Making Night Garden Blocks

1. To aid in joining the hexagons together, use the seam line template on page 14 to mark the seam allowances on the wrong side of each fabric hexagon. Stitch the hexagon flowers together either by hand or by machine, as follows: Join the first three hexagons to the center yellow hexagon right sides together, sewing from raw edge to raw edge.

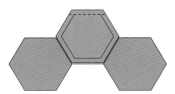

2. Add the last three hexagons to the yellow center, stitching from seam allowance to seam allowance. Press the seam allowances toward the yellow center.

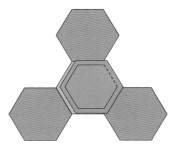

3. Sew the six outer hexagons to each other, stitching from the inner seam allowance to the outer raw edge.

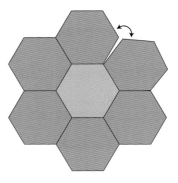

4. Add the two hexagon leaves, stitching from the inside corners to the outer raw edge. Press the seam allowances toward the green leaves.

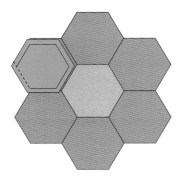

5. Turn under and press a ¼" seam allowance around the edge of the flower. Appliqué the flower to the center of a black background rectangle. Make four blocks, using a different bright for each one.

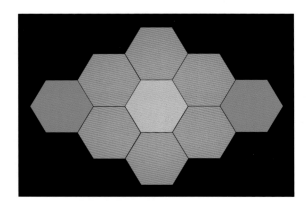

Making the Sashing Units

1. Pair each of the bright-print 2½" x 42" strips with a black multi-print 2½" x 42" strip. Sew each pair of strips right sides together. Press the seam allowances toward the black print. Make six strip-sets.

2. Cut the strip-sets into 2½" two-patch units.

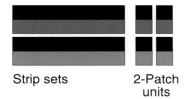

Strip sets   2-Patch units

3. Sew any 10 two-patch units together to create one checkerboard sashing strip. Make four of these. Join any seven two-patch units to create one checkerboard strip. Make two of these. Arrange two two-patch units into one four-patch cornerstone for the sashing. Make seven cornerstones.

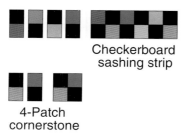

Checkerboard
sashing strip

4-Patch
cornerstone

4. Sew the Night Garden blocks, solid sashings, checkerboard sashings, and cornerstones together in two vertical rows, following the quilt assembly diagram on page 14.

5. For the inner border, sew five 1" x 42" black strips end to end. Measure the quilt top through the center from top to bottom. Cut two strips that length and sew one to each side of the quilt top. Press the seam allowances toward the black. Measure the quilt top through the center from side to side. Cut two strips that length and sew these to the top and bottom of the quilt top. Press the seam allowances toward the black.

6. For the outer border, join the remaining 4½" pink strips end to end. Measure the quilt top through the center from top to bottom. Cut two pink strips that length and sew one to each side of the quilt top. Press the seam allowances toward the pink.

7. Sew an orange 2½" x 20½" strip lengthwise to a green 2½" x 20½" strip and cut this strip-set into eight 2½" two-patch units. Sew the units into four four-patch units for the corner squares.

8. Join the 4½" blue strips end-to-end. Measure the quilt top through the center from side to side. Cut two blue strips that length. Sew one corner square to each end of both blue strips, and sew these to the top and bottom of the quilt top. Press the seam allowances toward the border.

Finishing Your Quilt

1. Layer the quilt top, batting, and backing. Then baste the layers together and quilt as desired.

2. Sew your binding strips together end-to-end. Fold the long binding strip in half lengthwise, wrong sides together, and press the fold line.

3. Place the raw edges of the binding against the raw edges on top of the quilt. Sew with a ¼" seam allowance. Turn the folded edge to the back and stitch it in place.

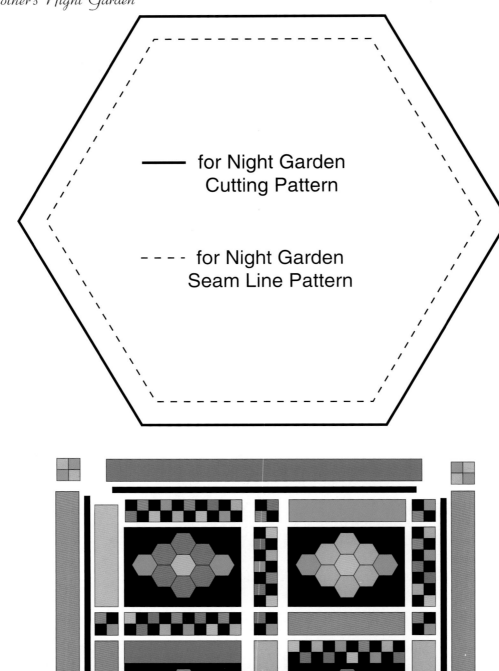

—— for Night Garden
Cutting Pattern

- - - - for Night Garden
Seam Line Pattern

GRANDMOTHER'S NIGHT GARDEN Quilt Assembly

Jeweled Keepsake Hearts

Jewel tones on a pumpkin orange background are an adventure in color not often taken. The eye-popping result is sassy and bold. I imagine the hearts dancing across the face of this quilt in sheer delight as they break out of the ordinary.

Quilt size 32" x 42"
Block size 8" x 8"

Materials and Cutting Guide

Use fabrics at least 42" wide. All strips are cut across the width of the fabric unless stated otherwise.

Materials	First Cut	Second Cut
template material	1 template from Heart pattern on page 17	
paper-backed fusible webbing, 1 yd	36 squares 3⅞"	
bright jewel-tone prints, 36 scraps	1 square 4" from each fabric for hearts	
pumpkin-orange, ⅞ yd (or ½ yd each of two different pumpkin-orange)	3 strips 8½" x 42"	12 squares 8½" for block backgrounds
bright multi-print with black in it, ¾ yd	8 strips 2½" x 42"	31 rectangles 2½" x 8½" for sashing
black solid, ½ yd	2 strips 2½" x 42" 4 strips 2" x 42" for binding	20 squares 2½" for cornerstones
backing, 1½ yd	36" x 46"	
batting	36" x 46"	

Making Heart Blocks

1. Center a 3⅞" square of fusible webbing on the wrong side of each 4" square. Use a pressing sheet between the fabric square and your ironing board cover, and another sheet between your block and the iron. Press with a hot iron and allow to cool. (Be sure to read the manufacturer's instructions for your fusible webbing.)

2. Trace around the heart template onto the paper side of the webbing. Cut out the hearts but don't remove the paper until you are ready to work on each block.

3. Select three hearts with good contrast between them, peel off the paper backing, and arrange them on an 8½" background square. Protect your iron and ironing board with pressing sheets. Press with a hot iron and allow to cool. Fuse 12 blocks.

4. Appliqué the hearts to the background blocks using black thread and a buttonhole stitch. Practice on a sample block or scrap block to get the buttonhole stitch the way you want it.

5. Sew three blocks and four sashing strips, beginning and ending with the sashing strips. Make four of these horizontal rows.

6. Sew together four black squares with three sashing strips, beginning and ending with the black squares. Make five of these.

7. Sew the quilt top together according to the JEWELED KEEPSAKE HEARTS quilt assembly diagram below.

JEWELED KEEPSAKE HEARTS Quilt Assembly

Finishing Your Quilt

1. Layer the quilt top, batting, and backing. Then baste the layers together and quilt as desired.

2. Sew your binding strips together end-to-end. Fold the binding strip in half lengthwise, wrong sides together, and press the fold line.

3. Place the raw edges of the binding against the raw edges on top of the quilt. Sew with a ¼" seam allowance. Turn the folded edge to the back and stitch it in place.

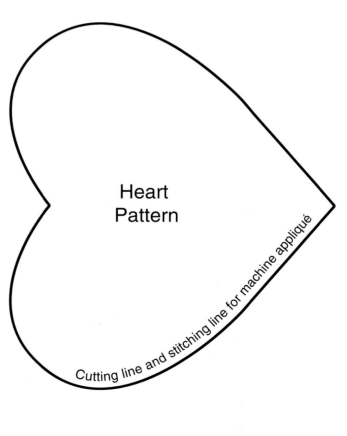

Heart
Pattern

Cutting line and stitching line for machine appliqué

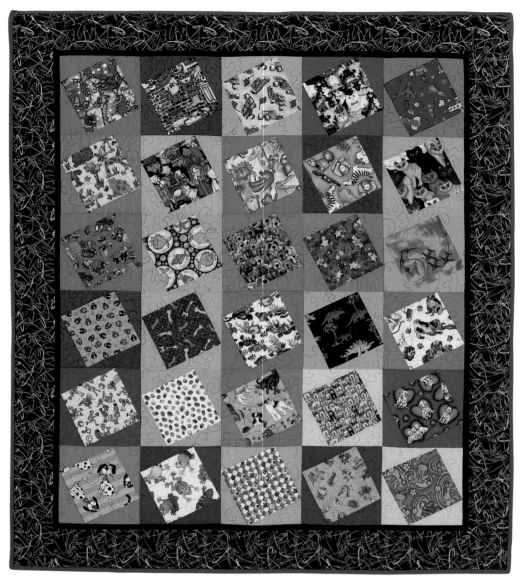

TALKING QUILT, 45" x 52", made by the author

Talking Quilt

Quilt size 45½" x 52½"
Block size 7¼" x 7¼"

A child's nap time is never lonely when he or she has a talking quilt. The use of novelty prints for kids provides all the interest needed to study the lively images until the sleepy-time fairy gently shuts their eyes for a short journey to dreamland.

Materials and Cutting Guide

Use fabrics at least 42" wide. All strips are cut across the width unless otherwise stated.

Materials	Cuts
template material	1 template from Setting Triangle pattern on page 21
novelty prints, 30 scraps	1 square 6" each
30 bright solids, ⅛ yd each	1 strip 3¼" x 42" from each for block backgrounds
black solid, ¼ yd	6 lengthwise strips 1" x 54" for inner border (pieced)
black multi-print, 1⅝ yd	4 lengthwise strips 4½" x 54" for outer border
red print, ⅜ yd	5 strips 2" x 42" for binding
backing, 3 yd	49" x 56" (pieced)
batting	49" x 56"

Making Talking Blocks

1. From each bright solid, cut setting triangles from the template on page 21. Important: all cutting is done from the right side of the fabric, because the angle of the template remains the same for all four setting triangles.

2. Sew one setting triangle to each side of a novelty-print square, matching the long sides of the triangle to the sides of the square. Press each seam allowance toward the triangle as you sew. Make 30 blocks.

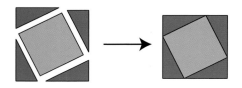

3. Sew five blocks together in a row to make six rows. Press all of the seam allowances

4. Sew the rows together according to the TALKING QUILT quilt assembly diagram on page 20. Press all of the seam allowances.

Finishing Your Quilt

1. For the inner border, measure the quilt from side to side through the center. Cut two inner-border strips to that length and sew these to the top and bottom of the quilt top. Press the seam allowances toward the border.

Talking Quilt

2. Measure the quilt from top to bottom through the center. Cut the remaining two inner-border strips to that length and sew one to each side of the quilt top. Press the seam allowances toward the border.

3. Repeat steps 1 and 2 to add the outer border. Press the seam allowances toward the border.

4. Layer the quilt top, batting, and backing. Then baste the layers together and quilt as desired.

5. Sew your binding strips together end-to-end. Fold the binding strip in half lengthwise, wrong sides together, and press the fold line.

6. Place the raw edges of the binding against the raw edges on top of the quilt. Sew with a ¼" seam allowance. Turn the folded edge to the back and stitch it in place.

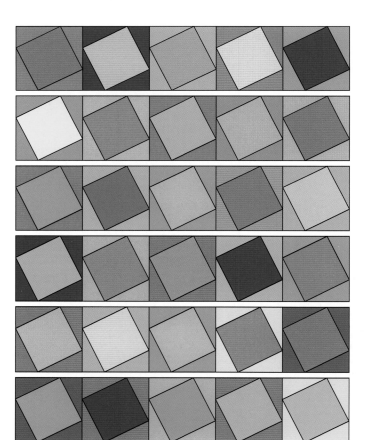

TALKING QUILT Quilt Assembly

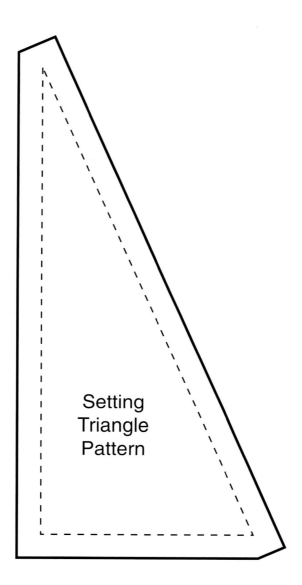

Setting
Triangle
Pattern

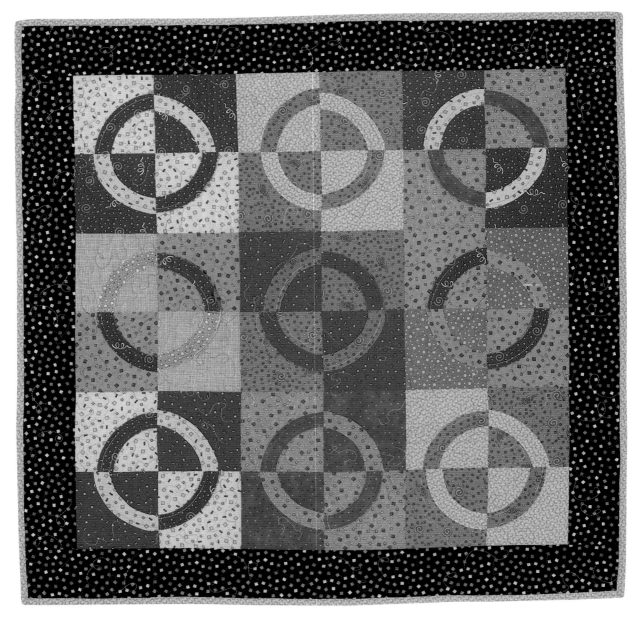

Fair Play

Quilt size 37" x 37"
Block size 10" x 10"

I found this block in the Ladies Art Company catalog from the early 1900s. I gave it an updated treatment with a quarter-circle template and raw-edge appliqué for quick cutting and piecing. I spanned 100 years of quilting tradition in just a few hours of sewing for a bright and sassy play quilt for a lucky child.

Materials and Cutting Guide

Use fabrics at least 42" wide. All strips are cut across the width of the fabric unless stated otherwise.

Materials	Cuts
template material	1 template from the Quarter Circle pattern on page 25
9 bright prints	1 square 8" from each print for donut shapes
9 bright prints	1 square 11" from each bright print for block background
black multi-print, ⅜ yd	4 strips 4" x 42" for border
green print, ½ yd	4 strips 2" x 42" for binding
backing, 1¼ yd	41" x 41"
batting	41" x 41"

Play Blocks

1. Fold each 11" square into fourths, and finger press the folds (do not iron). Set aside.

2. Fold each 8" square of fabric into fourths, finger pressing the folds. Align the Quarter Circle template along the two folds, as shown, and cut out a "donut" shape. Cut out nine of these.

3. Using the folds as a guide, center one fabric donut shape on one 11" square of a contrasting print. Press lightly with a warm iron, then pin the shape in place (or use small dabs of fabric glue).

4. Sew the donut shape to the square, stitching ¼" in from the inside and outside raw edges of the shape. Make nine units.

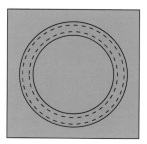

5. Cut each unit into quarters. Each quarter unit will be a 5½" square for a total of 36 quarter units.

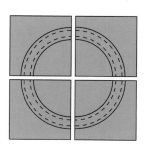

6. Sew together contrasting quarter units or mix and match units any way you like. Make nine Fair Play blocks.

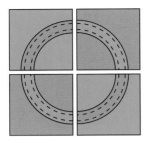

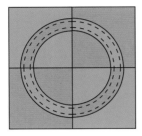

7. Sew three rows of three blocks according to the FAIR PLAY quilt assembly diagram on page 25. Press all of the seam allowances.

Finishing Your Quilt

1. For the border, measure the quilt from side to side through the center. Cut two border strips to that length and sew these to the top and bottom of the quilt top. Press the seam allowances toward the border.

2. Measure the quilt from top to bottom through the center. Cut the remaining two border strips to that length and sew one to each side of the quilt top. Press the seam allowances toward the black border.

3. Layer the quilt top, batting, and backing. Then baste the layers together and quilt as desired.

4. Sew your binding strips together end-to-end. Fold the binding strip in half lengthwise, wrong sides together, and press the fold line.

5. Place the raw edges of the binding against the raw edges on top of the quilt. Sew with a ¼" seam allowance. Turn the folded edge to the back and stitch in place.

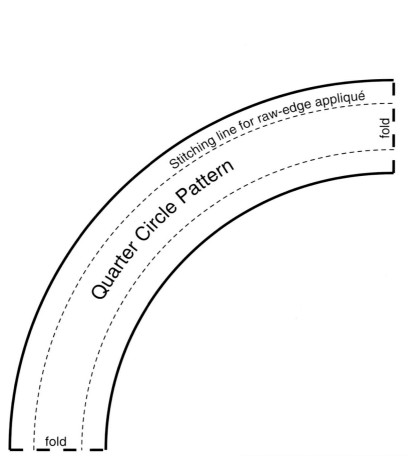

Stitching line for raw-edge appliqué

Quarter Circle Pattern

fold

fold

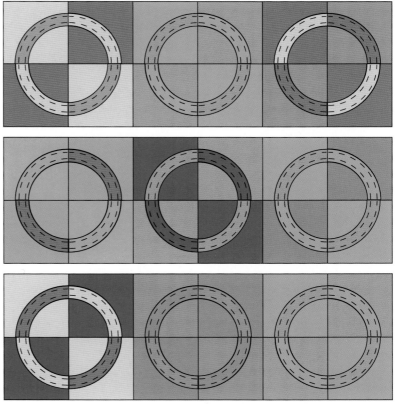

FAIR PLAY Quilt Assembly

98 Bright Dancing Squares, 40" x 40", made by the author.

98 Bright Dancing Squares

Quilt size 40" x 40"
Block size 5" x 5"

I began with an image of a rug I saw with squares edged in shimmering yellow. A lot of gold rayon thread adds sparkle to these fabric solids and seems to make the squares dance across the quilt.

Bold, Black & Beautiful Quilts ■■■ Debby Kratovil

Materials and Cutting Guide

Use fabrics at least 42" wide. All strips are cut across the width unless otherwise stated.

Materials	Cuts
10 or more solids, ¼ yd each	49 squares 5½" for block backgrounds 49 squares 3" for appliqué
black solid, ½ yd	4 strips 2" x 42" for outer border 5 squares 5½" for block backgrounds 5 squares 3" for appliqué
bright print, ½ yd	4 strips 1¼" x 42" for inner border 4 strips 2" x 42" for binding
backing, 1½ yd	44" x 44" (pieced)
batting	44" x 44"
gold rayon thread	
plain newsprint for tear-off stabilizer	49 squares 5"

Making Dancing Blocks

1. Pair 25 large squares with 25 small squares, mixing the colors to create a strong contrast within each pair. Fold and finger-press the horizontal and vertical centers of each square.

2. Center a small square inside a large square, using the finger-pressed creases to help with the alignment. Pin the small square in place. Use gold thread and a satin stitch to machine appliqué the small square to the large square, then press. On the wrong side, trim away the background fabric from behind the appliquéd square. Make 25 of these blocks.

3. Pair the remaining 24 large and small squares, again mixing the colors for contrast. Finger-press each square as you did in step 1.

4. Center one small square diagonally (on point) inside one large square, using the finger-pressed creases to help with the alignment. Pin the squares and appliqué with gold thread. On the wrong side, trim away the background fabric from behind the smaller appliquéd square. Make 24 of these blocks.

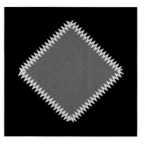

5. Sew together seven blocks horizontally, alternating between the squares set on point and the squares set upright. Begin every other row with the first block set upright. Make seven rows.

6. Sew the rows together according to the 98 BRIGHT DANCING SQUARES quilt assembly diagram below.

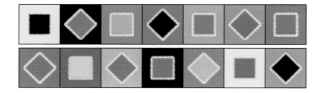

Finishing Your Quilt

1. For the black inner border, measure the quilt from side to side through the center. Cut two inner-border strips to that length and sew these to the top and bottom of the quilt top. Press the seam allowances toward the border.

2. Measure the quilt from top to bottom through the center. Cut the remaining two inner-border strips to that length and sew these to either side of the quilt top. Press the seam allowances toward the border.

3. Repeat steps 1 and 2 to add the outer print border. Press the seam allowances toward the border.

4. Layer the quilt top, batting, and backing. Then baste the layers together and quilt as desired.

5. Sew the binding strips together end-to-end. Fold the binding strip in half lengthwise, wrong sides together, and press the fold line.

6. Place the raw edges of the binding against the raw edges on top of the quilt. Sew with a ¼" seam allowance. Turn the folded edge to the back and stitch it in place.

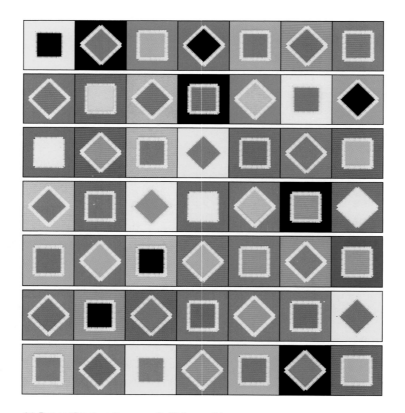

98 BRIGHT DANCING SQUARES Quilt Assembly

Velvet Stars

A tattered velveteen-backed pillow at a yard sale caught my eye one lazy summer Saturday. The colors in the needlepoint were bright and cheery and were stitched in a pattern similar to the one in this quilt.

Quilt size 48" x 62"
Block size: 12" x 12"

Materials and Cutting Guide

Use fabrics at least 42" wide. All strips are cut across the width unless stated otherwise.

Materials	First Cut	Second Cut
template material	1 template each from Velvet Star patterns A, B, and C on page 33	
10 to 12 bright solids, ⅛ yd of each	1 strip 4" x 42" from each color for star blocks 6 squares 2½" in green, as shown in the photo on page 29, or in a variety of colors for cornerstones	
multi-print, 1⅝ yd	4 lengthwise strips 4½" x 58½" for outer border	
multi-print with black, ⅝ yd	6 strips 2½" x 42"	17 strips 2½" x 12½" for sashings
stripe, ½ yd	6 strips 2" x 42" for binding	
backing, 3 yd	52" x 66" (pieced)	
batting	52" x 66"	

Making Star Blocks

1. Each block has four units made from different pairs of contrasting colors. Mix the colors in the units to make the most of contrast between colors.

2. Select two pairs of contrasting colors. From the first color, cut one 3½" square and two pieces from template C. From the second color, cut one piece from template A and one piece from template C. Sew the pieces together as shown. Make one unit.

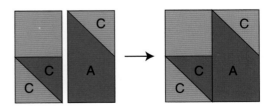

3. Repeat step 2 to make another unit with Star templates A and C from two new colors.

4. Select two more pairs of contrasting colors. From the first color, cut one 3½" square and two pieces from template C. From the second

color, cut one piece from template A and one piece from template B. Sew the pieces together as shown. Make one unit.

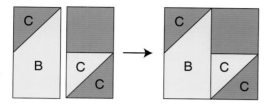

5. Repeat step 4 to make another unit with templates B and C from two new colors.

6. Sew the block according to the diagram below. Notice that the square pieces are on the outside corners and the A and B pieces are mirror images of each other. Make 12 blocks.

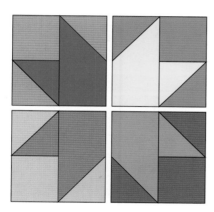

7. Sew three star blocks to two sashing strips, beginning and ending with the blocks. Make four of these horizontal rows.

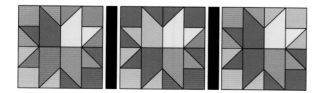

8. Sew three sashing strips to two sashing squares, beginning and ending with the sashing strips. Make three of these rows.

9. Sew the quilt top according to the VELVET STARS quilt assembly diagram on page 32.

Finishing Your Quilt

1. For the border, measure the quilt from side to side through the center. Cut two border strips to that length and sew these to the top and bottom of the quilt top. Press the seam allowances toward the border.

2. Sew the remaining border strips together end-to-end. Measure the quilt from top to bottom through the center. Cut two border strips to that length and sew one to each side of the quilt top. Press the seam allowances toward border.

3. Layer the quilt top, batting, and backing. Baste the layers together and quilt as desired.

4. Sew the binding strips together end-to-end. Fold the strip in half lengthwise, wrong sides together, and press the fold line.

5. Place the raw edges of the binding against the raw edges on top of the quilt. Sew with a ¼" seam allowance. Turn the folded edge to the back and stitch in place.

Velvet Stars

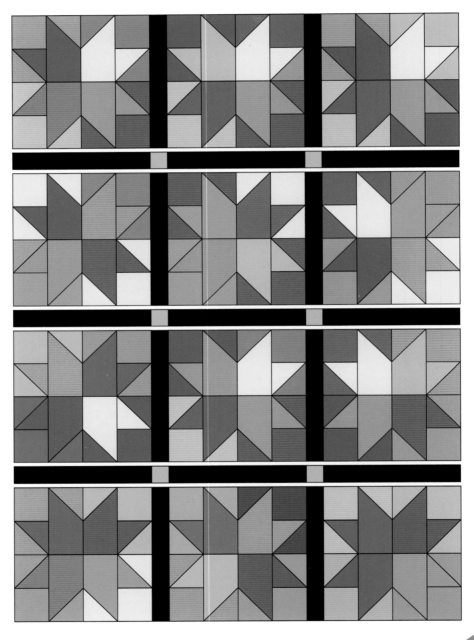

VELVET STARS Quilt Assembly

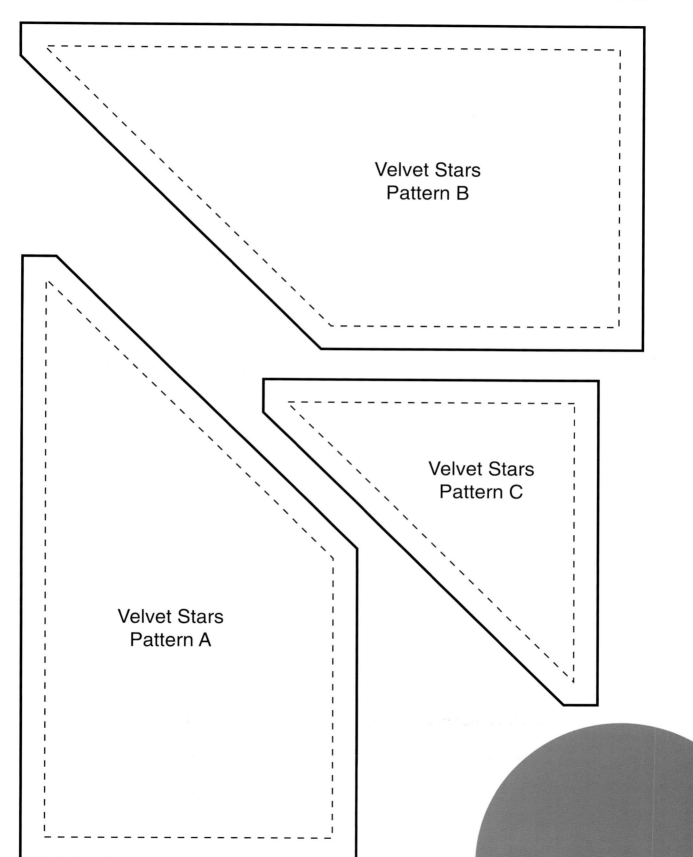

Velvet Stars
Pattern B

Velvet Stars
Pattern C

Velvet Stars
Pattern A

Autumn Tessellating Stars

Quit size 58" x 58"
Block size 12" x 12"

The inspiration for this quilt came from Islamic tile designs. In fact, many of these centuries-old patterns can be reinterpreted in cloth. If you can sew a straight line, you can recreate your own tessellating stars quilt.

Materials and Cutting Guide

Use fabrics at least 42" wide. All strips are cut across the width unless stated otherwise.

Materials	First Cut	Second Cut
black-on-black textured print, 1½ yd	4 strips 4½" x 42" for stars 4 strips 6½ " x 42"" for stars	64 rectangles 2½" x 4½" 64 rectangles 2½" x 6½"
leaf multi-print, 1½ yd	4 strips 4½" x 42" for block background 4 strips 6½" x 42" for block background	64 strips 2½" x 4½" 64 strips 2½" x 6½"
red, ¾ yd	5 strips 1" x 42" for inner border	
green multi-print, 2 yd	4 lengthwise strips 5½" x 67" for outer border 5 lengthwise strips 2" x 67" for binding	
backing, 3¾ yd	63" x 63" (pieced)	
batting	63" x 63"	

Making Star Blocks

1. Place one 2½" x 4½" black-on-black rectangle on top of one 2½" x 4½" leaf multi-print rectangle at right angles, right sides together. Sew along the diagonal (a), trim away the excess (b), and press (c). Make four two-color units.

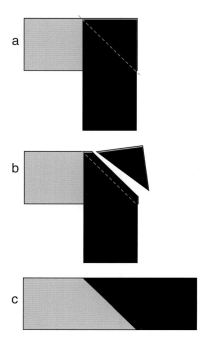

2. Sew together one leaf multi-print, one two-color unit, and one black-on-black unit. Press the seam allowances toward the black strips. Make four units.

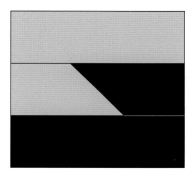

3. Sew four units together, as shown. Make 16 blocks.

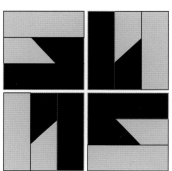

4. Sew four rows of four blocks, then sew the rows together according to the Autumn Tessellating Stars quilt assembly diagram on page 37.

Finishing Your Quilt

1. For the inner border, sew the strips together end to end. Measure the quilt from side to side through the center. Cut two inner-border strips to that length and sew these to the top and bottom of the quilt top. Press the seam allowances toward the border.

2. Measure the quilt from top to bottom through the center. Cut the remaining two inner-border strips to that length and sew one to each side of the quilt top. Press the seam allowances toward the border.

3. Repeat steps 1 and 2 to add the outer border. Press the seam allowances toward the border.

4. Layer the quilt top, batting, and backing. Then baste the layers together and quilt as desired.

5. Sew your binding strips together end-to-end. Fold the binding strip in half lengthwise, wrong sides together, and press the fold line.

6. Place the raw edges of the binding against the raw edges on top of the quilt. Sew with a ¼" seam allowance. Turn the folded edge to the back and stitch it in place.

AUTUMN TESSELLATING STARS Quilt Assembly

SHOTGUN WEDDING RING, 51" x 66", made by Susan Fisher, Kennesaw, Georgia. Machine quilted by Michelle Wyman, Acworth, Georgia.

Shotgun
Wedding Ring

This is my quick and easy method for making a wedding ring quilt. Machine appliqué makes this a speedy rendition of the traditional block. Susan Fisher made this for a friend who preferred an asymmetric arrangement of the colors in the rings.

Quilt size 51" x 66"
Block size 15" x 15"

Materials and Cutting Guide

Use fabrics at least 42" wide. All strips are cut across the width unless stated otherwise.

Materials	First Cut	Second Cut
template material	1 template from the Ring pattern on page 41	
black, 4 yd	12 strips 8½" x 42" 6 strips 2" x 42" for binding	48 squares 8½" for block backgrounds
bright green, 1 yd	Fit the ring template end-to-end across the width of the fabric to trace and cut 24 rings	
bright pink, 1 yd	Fit the ring template end-to-end across the width of the fabric to trace and cut 24 rings	
backing, 3¼ yd	55" x 73" (pieced)	
batting	55" x 73"	

Making Ring Blocks

1. Fold a black 8½" square once on the diagonal and lightly press a crease in it. Use this as a guideline to center and pin one bright pink ring to the black square.

2. With a matching pink thread, appliqué the ring unit to the square using a small zigzag stitch around the inside and outside raw edges of the ring.

3. Trim each block to 8" x 8" taking care to leave a ¼" seam allowance from the tip of the ring to the corner of the square. Make 24 bright pink ring blocks.

4. Repeat the first three steps to appliqué 24 bright green ring blocks using matching green thread.

5. Arrange groups of four blocks with the rings pointing outward or inward, depending on how you plan to lay out your quilt. See the SHOTGUN WEDDING RING quilt assembly diagrams on page 40 for some ideas. Make 12 block sets.

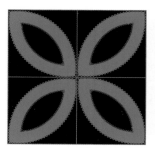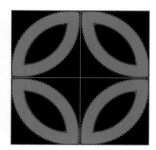

6. Layout and sew three block sets to a row in a pattern of your own choosing. (See the SHOTGUN WEDDING RING quilt diagram on page 40

for some possible arrangements that make symmetrical designs.)

7. Press the seam allowances in the even-numbered and odd-numbered rows in opposite directions. Sew the rows together, and press.

Finishing Your Quilt

1. Layer the quilt top, batting, and backing. Then baste the layers together and quilt as desired.

2. Sew the binding strips together end-to-end. Fold the binding strip in half lengthwise, wrong sides together, and press the fold line.

3. Place the raw edges of binding against the raw edges on top of the quilt. Sew with a ¼" seam allowance. Turn the folded edge to the back and stitch it in place.

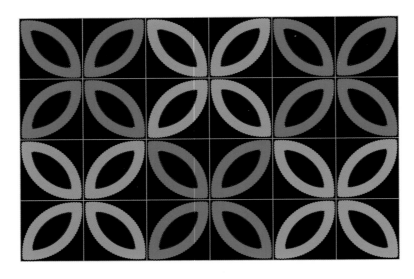

SHOTGUN WEDDING RING Quilt Assembly

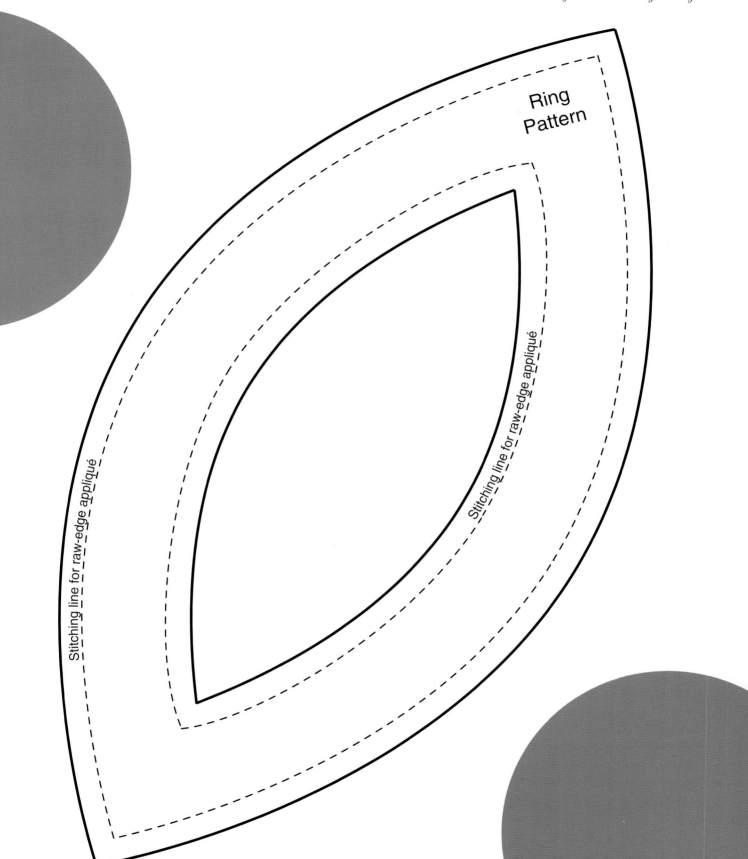

Ring
Pattern

Stitching line for raw-edge appliqué

Stitching line for raw-edge appliqué

GOLDEN MARINER'S COMPASS, 23½" x 23½", made by the author

Golden Mariner's Compass

Quilt size 23" x 23"
Block size 14" x 14"

The deep, rich colors of black, red, and gold reflect the trees of autumn. The colors in this Mariner's Compass take their cues from the leaves.

Materials and Cutting Guide

Use fabric at least 42" wide. All strips are cut across the width unless stated otherwise.

Materials	First Cut	Second Cut
Quarter Compass paper foundation on page 45	Trace or photocopy to make 4 paper foundations	
Quarter Circle pattern on page 45	Trace onto paper folded into quarters	
red, 1 fat quarter	1 strip 4½" x 21" 1 strip 7⅞" x 21"	4 rectangles 3½" x 4½" for piece #1 2 squares 7⅞ for background
yellow, ¼ yd	1 strip 4½" x 42"	8 squares 4½" for pieces #2 and #3
orange, 1 fat eighth	1 strip 6" x 21"	4 rectangles 2½" x 6" for piece #4
black, 1 fat quarter	1 strip 6" x 21" 1 strip 7⅞" x 21"	4 rectangles 2½" x 6" for piece #5 2 squares 7⅞" for background
gold, scrap	1 square 5½" for compass center	
burnt orange, ¼ yd	4 strips 1¼" x 42" for inner border	
leaf print, ¾ yd	4 strips 4¼" x 42" for outer border 4 strips 2" x 42" for binding	
backing, 1 yd	28" x 28"	
batting	28" x 28"	

Making Compass Quarter Blocks

1. Use four copies of the Quarter Compass paper foundation. Take note that you are sewing on the printed side of the pattern which is the mirror image of the finished block. The colors are labeled on the paper foundation to correspond with the quilt diagram on page 45.

2. Piece each quarter block in the order shown on the template. Be sure to include the ¼" outer seam allowances in your piecing. Trim any excess from the seam allowances.

Take note that the colors in the paper-foundation pattern are asymmetric. As a result, the orange and black in the star points in your final pieced block will be the mirror image of the way they are labeled on the pattern.

3. Sew the four quarter units together as shown below. Press the seams open.

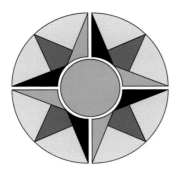

4. Fold a large piece of paper into fourths. Trace the Quarter Circle pattern onto the paper, aligning the folds as shown on the pattern. With the pattern folded, cut out the circle. Use this paper pattern to cut out the center of the block. Then appliqué the circle to the center of your block.

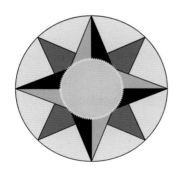

5. Draw a line along one diagonal of the back of the 7⅞" red squares. Place one red and one black square right sides together and stitch ¼" along both sides of the drawn line. Cut along the drawn line and press the triangles toward the black fabric. Repeat this step to yield four half-square triangle units. Stitch them together as shown below.

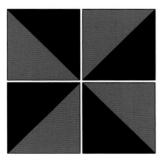

6. Appliqué the compass to the red and black background according to the GOLDEN MARINER'S COMPASS quilt assembly diagram on page 45. On the wrong side of your block, trim away the background fabric from behind the appliquéd compass.

Finishing Your Quilt

1. For the inner border, measure the quilt from side to side through the center. Cut two burnt orange inner-border strips to that length and sew these to the top and bottom of the quilt top. Press the seam allowances toward the border.

2. Measure the quilt from top to bottom through the center. Cut the remaining two burnt orange inner-border strips to that length and sew one to each side of the quilt top. Press the seam allowances toward border.

3. Repeat steps 1 and 2 to add the outer border. Press the seam allowances toward the border.

4. Layer the quilt top, batting, and backing. Then baste the layers together and quilt as desired.

5. Sew your binding strips together end-to-end. Fold the binding strip in half lengthwise, wrong sides together, and press the fold line.

6. Place the raw edges of the binding against the raw edges on top of the quilt. Sew with a ¼" seam allowance. Turn the folded edge to the back and stitch it in place.

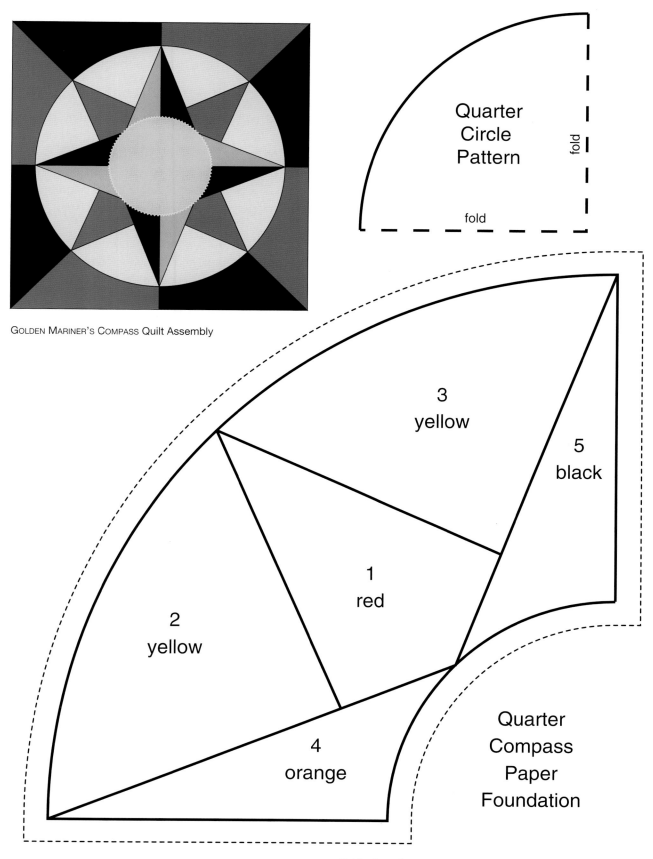

GOLDEN MARINER'S COMPASS Quilt Assembly

Quarter
Circle
Pattern

fold

fold

3
yellow

5
black

1
red

2
yellow

4
orange

Quarter
Compass
Paper
Foundation

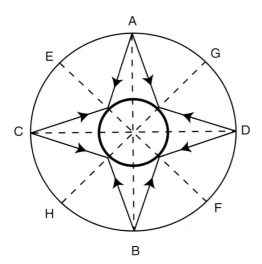

Diagram 1

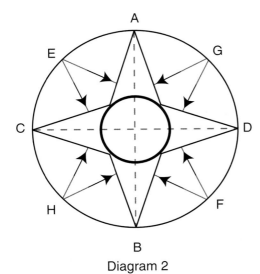

Diagram 2

Diagram 3

Coffee Filter Mariner's Compass

A large coffee filter has an approximate diameter of 9½".

Press a coffee filter smooth with a warm iron and fold it into equal-sized halves, quarters, and eighths as indicated by the dashed lines A–H. Your circle will be divided into eight equal-sized wedges with an internal angle of 45 degrees. Use a pen or pencil to draw in these lines.

Find a 3" lid from a jar or juice can (or anything around your house that comes close to a 3" diameter). Trace it onto a piece of freezer paper and cut it out. Center it over the coffee filter circle and trace around it as shown in diagram 1. Take a ruler and connect Point A to the edge of the small circle where it intersects Line EF and Line GH. The arrows on the two lines originating at A illustrate this. Connect Point C to the edge of the small circle where it intersects Line EF and Line GH. Continue as shown, connecting Point B to Line GH and Line EF; and Point D to Line GH and Line EF. Continue to draw compass points E–H in the same manner, as shown in diagram 2.

Diagram 3 illustrates one quarter unit separated from the others. The numbered pieces can either be cut apart and used as templates (adding ¼" seam allowance to each), or you can foundation piece the quadrant/quarter circle right on the paper.

How to handle the large center circle? I leave that for the last. After I piece the four quadrants, I then stitch them together to make the large circle. I appliqué the smaller circle to the center, trimming the excess fabric from underneath.

ROYAL STAR, 49" x 49", made by the author

Royal Star

Stars shine their brightest against an ebony night sky. I had a packet of bright mottled prints that just begged me to make them into vibrant stars. I chose a traditional block and set it with the solid black fabric, then added extra strips to make these stars float in the heavens. Paper piecing the star points guarantees perfect points.

Quilt size 49" x 49"
Block size 8½" x 8½"

Materials and Cutting Guide

Use fabrics at least 42" wide. All strips are cut across the width unless stated otherwise.

Important note: To simplify this project, and to give you choices when you lay out your quilt top, the amounts given in the cutting and sewing instructions yield more cornerstones than you will actually need for your quilt.

Materials	First Cut	Second Cut
64 copies of Corner Unit paper piecing pattern on page 51 (use 4 paper foundations for each block.)		
black solid, 2½ yds	6 strips 3¼" x 42"	64 squares 3¼" for piece #1
	4 strips 5¼" x 42"	32 squares 5¼" for pieces 4 and 5, each square cut twice on the diagonal
	10 strips 1½" x 42" for sashing	8 strips 1½" x 13 and 16 strips 1½" x 7" for cornerstones
	6 strips 1½" x 42"	
	6 strips 2" x 42" for binding	
8 bright prints, ½ yd each	3 strips 2½" x 42" from each of 8 brights	16 strips 2½" x 3¼" for star points (makes 2 blocks) and 18 squares 2½" x 2½" for block centers (makes 2 sets of Color 1 block centers and 2 sets of Color 2 centers, shown on page 49)
	1 strip 1½" x 42" from each of 8 brights	2 strips 1½" x 13" from each bright and 1 strip 1½" x 7" for cornerstones (makes 4 from each bright)
	2 strips 1½" x 42" from each of 2 brights	
	1 strip 1½" x 42 from each of 6 brights for sashing	
backing, 3 yd	54" x 54" (pieced)	
batting	54" x 54"	

Making Star Blocks

1. Pin or fabric glue a 3¼" black square to the non-printed side of the paper foundation in position #1, overlapping the printed seam lines by ½" all around.

2. Place a 2½" x 3¼" strip for piece #2 on piece #1, right sides together. From the printed side of the paper foundation, stitch along the printed line. Trim the seam allowance to a uniform ¼".

3. Fold piece #2 over, wrong side to the paper foundation, and press the seam line. Add remaining pieces #3, #4, and #5 in the same manner in numerical order. Make four corner units.

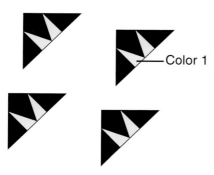

4. Sew the nine-patch unit for your block, using four 2½" squares from the same fabric as your star points, and five 2½" squares from a contrasting bright print. Make 16 Nine-Patch units.

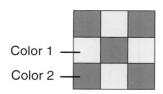

5. Assemble your Royal Star blocks according to the following diagram. Make 16 blocks.

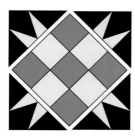

Important pressing tip: Press the seam allowances toward the star points. Joining the seams of the corner units with the Nine-Patch will be much easier, because the seams will butt up against each other.

Preparing the Sashing

1. To prepare one sashing unit, sew a 1½" x 42" black strip to each long side of one 1½" x 42" bright print strip. Press the seam allowances toward the black fabric. Make one to two strip-sets like this for each of the eight brights. Cut the strip-sets into 9" segments. Make a total of 40 black-bright-black sashing units.

2. Sew four Royal Star blocks and five sashing units together, beginning and ending with the sashing units. Make four of these four-block rows.

Making Nine-Patch Cornerstones

1. To make four Nine-Patch cornerstone units from one bright print, sew two 1½" x 13" bright print strips on each side of one 1½" x 13" black strip. Press seam allowances toward the black. Cut eight 1½" units from this strip-set.

2. Sew two 1½" x 7" black strips on each side of one 1½" x 7" bright print strip. Press seam allowances toward the black. Cut four 1½" units from this strip-set.

3. Assemble Nine-Patch cornerstones, positioning units so a bright print square is in the middle. Make four Nine-Patch cornerstones.

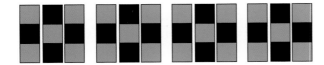

4. In the same manner, make four cornerstones from each of the eight bright strips, for a total of 32 cornerstones (you will have extra corner-stones).

5. Sew together five Nine-Patch cornerstones with four sashing units, beginning and ending with a Nine-Patch cornerstone. Make five of these sashing Nine-Patch units.

6. Sew the quilt top together according to the ROYAL STAR quilt assembly diagram below.

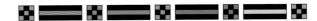

Finishing Your Quilt

1. Layer the quilt top, batting, and backing. Then baste the layers together and quilt as desired.

3. Sew the binding strips together end-to-end. Fold the resulting long binding strip in half lengthwise, wrong sides together, and press the fold line.

4. Place the raw edges of binding against the raw edges on top of the quilt. Sew with a ¼" seam allowance. Turn the folded edge to the back and sew it in place.

ROYAL STAR Quilt Assembly

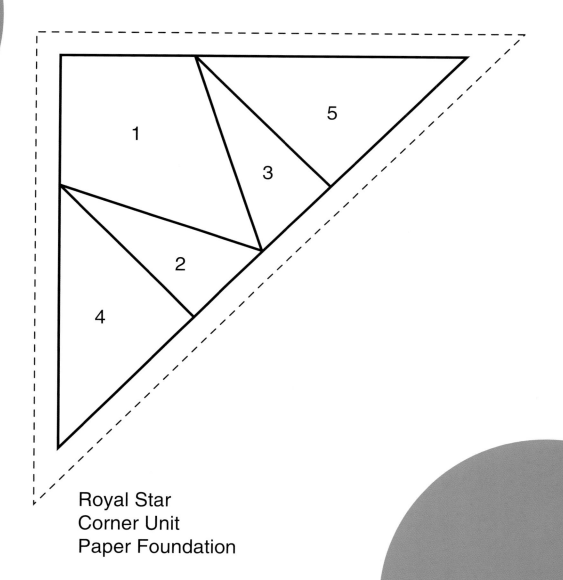

Royal Star
Corner Unit
Paper Foundation

MINI GRANDMA'S GARDEN, 31" x 31", made by the author

Mini Grandma's Garden

My little garden quilt began as a way to keep my hands busy while traveling. A friend gave me a packet of paper hexagons and a quick lesson on making English paper-pieced flowers. Placing the flowers onto larger squares allowed me to incorporate other bright, quick-cut patches into this cheery quilt.

Quilt size 31" x 31"
Block size 6" x 6"

Materials and Cutting Guide

Fabric	First Cut	Second Cut
template material	7 templates from Mini Garden pattern on page 55	
freezer paper (Optional; see instructions)	49 hexagons from Mini Garden template pattern	
black, ½ yd	2 strips 6½" x 42"	7 squares 6½" for block backgrounds
bright yellow, ¼ yd	2 squares 3⅞"	Cut each once on the diagonal for small setting triangles.
	2 squares 5⅛"	Cut each once on the diagonal for large setting triangles.
	7 pieces 2¾" x 3" for flower centers	
	4 strips 1" x 42" for inner border	
purple, ⅞ yd	2 squares 6⅞"	Cut each once on the diagonal for large setting triangles.
	2 squares 3½" for corner blocks	
	4 strips 3½" x 42" for outer border	
	4 strips 2" x 42" for binding	
bright pink, ⅛ yd	10 squares 3⅞" for blocks	Cut each once on the diagonal.
bright green, ⅛ yd	10 squares 3⅞" for blocks	Cut each once on the diagonal.
seven bright prints, ⅛ yd	6 pieces each 2¾" x 3" for flowers	
backing, 1⅛ yd	35" x 35"	
batting	35" x 35"	

English Paper Piecing

1. For one Mini Garden flower, use six 2¾" x 3" pieces from one bright print and one piece from the yellow fabric.

2. For the next step, you can use freezer paper templates cut from the Mini Garden pattern for each individual hexagon, or you can use templates cut from sturdy material. For easy removal later on, punch a hole in the center of each template using a paper punch.

3. Place a Mini Garden template on the wrong side of a 2¾" x 3" piece. Fold and press the fabric over the edges of the template, one side at a time around the template (in either a clockwise or counter-clockwise direction) taking

care that the fold of the fabric at each corner is sharp. Note: The wrong sides of the blocks will be messy.

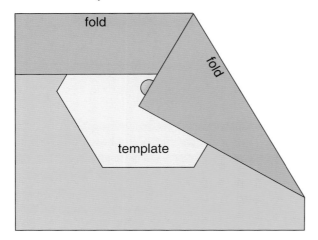

4. Baste the corners by slip stitching through the fabric at each fold, taking care not to catch the template. Keep your stitches ¼" from the template edges.

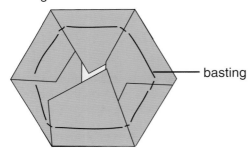

5. When you have several patches basted, they are ready to be joined. Place two patches right sides together and, using a single strand of cotton thread, sew with an overcast stitch. Try not to catch the paper but just a few threads from each patch. Sewing small, short stitches close together is the goal.

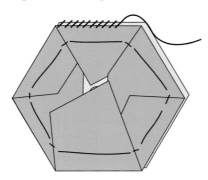

6. When two patches are joined together, open them out and finger press the seam flat. Now you can add the next patch.

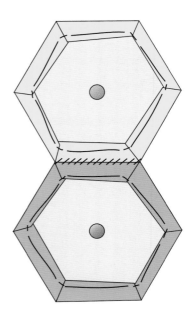

7. After joining all of the patches, trim the excess fabric to within ¼". Remove the paper templates and lightly press your work flat.

Making Garden Blocks

1. Center each flower on a 6½" black background square. Appliqué the flower in place by hand or machine.

2. On the wrong side of each block, trim away the black background fabric from behind the flower to reduce bulk and dark-color show through, then press again.

3. Sew two small yellow triangles to one purple square, then sew these to one purple triangle. Make two units.

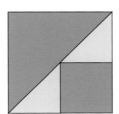

4. Sew two pink triangles to one green square. Make ten units.

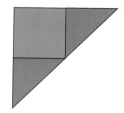

5. Sew the flower blocks and units together in diagonal rows as shown in the MINI GRANDMA'S GARDEN quilt assembly diagram below.

Finishing Your Quilt

1. For the inner border, measure the quilt top from side to side through the center. Cut two inner-border strips to that length and sew these to the top and bottom of the quilt top. Press the seam allowances toward the border.

2. Measure the quilt top from top to bottom through the center. Cut the remaining two inner-border strips to that length and sew one to each side of the quilt top. Press the seam allowances toward the border.

3. Repeat steps 1 and 2 to add the outer border. Press the seam allowances toward the purple.

4. Layer the quilt top, batting, and backing. Then baste the layers together and quilt as desired.

5. Sew your binding strips together end-to-end. Fold the binding strip in half lengthwise, wrong sides together, and press the fold line.

6. Place the raw edges of the binding against the raw edges on top of the quilt. Sew with a ¼" seam allowance. Turn the folded edge to the back and stitch it in place.

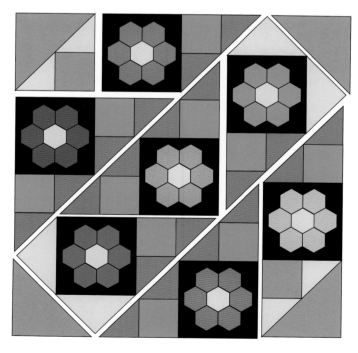

MINI GRANDMA'S GARDEN Quilt Assembly

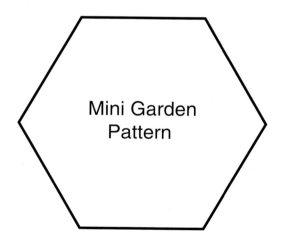

Mini Garden Pattern

BUTTERFLIES AT NIGHT, 35" x 47", made by the author

Butterflies at Night

A traditional Dresden Plate block with 12 blades was the start of this lucky set of butterflies. I mistakenly separated the Dresden Plate ring into three sections instead of two for another project. When I placed the sections side by side, I saw butterfly wings.

Quilt size 35" x 47"
Block size 10" x 10"

Materials and Cutting Guide

Use fabrics at least 42" wide. All strips are cut across the width unless stated otherwise.

Materials	First Cut	Second Cut
template material	1 template from Butterfly Wing pattern on page 60.	
black solid, ¾ yd	2 strips 10½" x 42" for block backgrounds	6 squares 10½"
	1 strip 2½" x 42" for sashing cornerstones	12 squares 2½"
bright print, ½ yd	17 strips 2½" x 10½" for sashing	
12 bright prints, ¼ yd (one pair of contrasting prints for each butterfly)	1 strip each fabric 4½" x 42" for butterfly wings	4 wedges from pattern on page 60
fat eighths or scraps of six different prints	1 strip each 2" x 5¼" for butterfly bodies	
bright yellow, ⅛ yd	4 strips 1" x 42" for inner border	
bright blue print, ⅝ yd	4 strips 4¼" x 42" for outer border	
yellow multi-print, ¼ yd	4 strips 2" x 42" for binding	
backing, 1⅝ yd	39" x 51"	
batting	39" x 51"	

Making a Butterfly Block

1. Select two contrasting bright prints. Cut four wedges from each fabric, using the Butterfly Wing template, on page 60. Cut six sets of wedges.

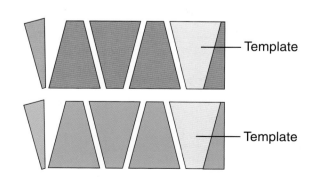

Template

Template

2. Working with one set of wedges at a time, fold a wedge in half lengthwise, right sides together, and stitch ¼" from the end as shown in (a). Clip away the tiny triangle of fabric (b). Fold the sewn tip out to the right side and press, taking care to center the seam (c). Sew six sets of butterfly wings.

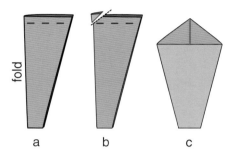

a   b   c

3. Work with one set of wedges at a time. Stitch together a butterfly wing from four wedges, alternating colors. Repeat for remaining four wedges, taking care to alternate the colors. Press all seams either one way or open.

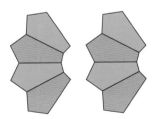

4. Finger press a black square in half twice. Using the finger-pressed folds as guides, align and center matching sets of butterfly wings onto the black background squares according to the block diagram below. Pin the wings in place with the raw edges of the wing units just touching, as shown. Make six butterfly blocks.

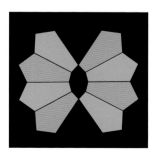

5. For the butterfly body, fold a 2" x 5¼" strip in half lengthwise, right sides together, and stitch a ¼" seam across both ends (a). Clip away tiny triangles of fabric (b). Then turn, and press (c), centering the seams as you did with the Dresden Plate wedges.

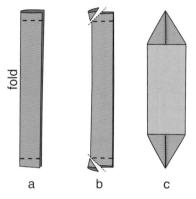

a   b   c

6. Turn under the raw edges of the two long sides ¼" and press. Make 6 butterfly bodies.

7. Select a contrasting butterfly body for one block. Center and pin one body over the two wings, taking care to cover the raw edges of the wings. Then appliqué your butterfly to the black background and press. Repeat for each block.

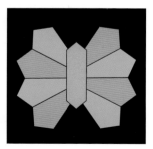

Preparing the Sashing

1. Sew a row with two butterfly blocks and three sashing strips, beginning and ending with the sashing strips. Make three of these two-block rows.

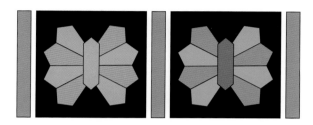

2. Sew together three black squares with two sashing units, beginning and ending with the squares. Press the seam allowances toward the black squares. Make four of these.

3. Sew your quilt top together according to the BUTTERFLIES AT NIGHT quilt assembly diagram at right.

Finishing Your Quilt

1. For the inner border, measure the quilt top from side to side through the center. Cut two yellow inner-border strips to that length and sew these to the top and bottom of the quilt top. Press the seam allowances toward the border.

2. Measure the quilt from top to bottom through the center. Cut the remaining two yellow inner-border strips to that length and sew one to each side of the quilt top. Press the seam allowances toward the border.

3. Repeat steps 1 and 2 to add the outer blue print border. Press the seam allowances toward the border.

4. Layer the quilt top, batting, and backing. Then baste the layers together and quilt as desired.

5. Sew the binding strips together end-to-end. Fold the binding strip in half lengthwise, wrong sides together, and press the fold line.

6. Place the raw edges of binding against the raw edges on top of the quilt. Sew with a ¼" seam allowance. Turn the folded edge to the back and stitch it in place.

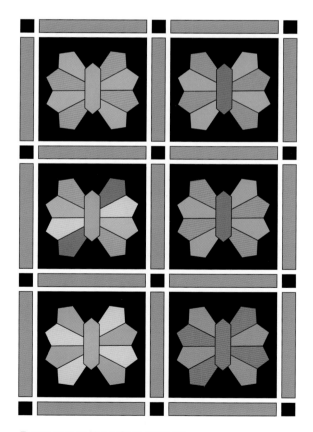

BUTTERFLIES AT NIGHT Quilt Assembly

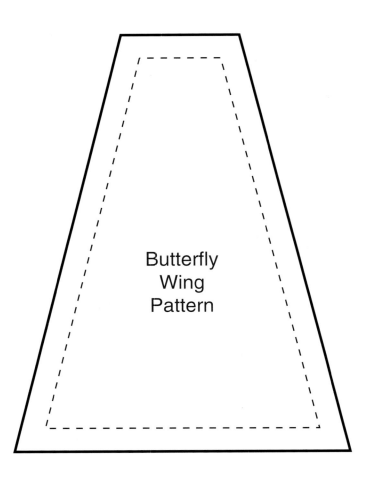

Butterfly
Wing
Pattern

PINK AND BLACK IRISH CHAIN, 31" x 31", made by the author

Pink and Black Irish Chain

This black and hot pink Double Irish Chain began with two small embroidery designs I created with my sewing machine. They fit snugly onto a 4½" background square. But when expanded with a little more fabric and patches of black and pink, they appear to float on a background of night.

Quilt size 31½" x 31½"
Block size 4½" x 4½"

Materials and Cutting Guide

Use fabrics at least 42" wide. All strips are cut across the width unless stated otherwise.

Materials	First Cut	Second Cut
pink embroidery floss		
black, ⅝ yd	1 strip 5" x 20" 6 strips 2" x 42"	4 squares 5" for embroidery blocks 5 strips 2" x 32" for Irish Chain blocks 16 rectangles 2" x 5" for sashing
hot pink, ½ yd	6 strips 2" x 42"	5 strips 2" x 32" for Irish Chain blocks 16 squares 2" for cornerstones
black floral print, ⅞ yd	4 strips 4½" x 42" for border 4 strips 2" x 42" for binding	
backing, 1⅛ yd	35" x 35"	
batting	35" x 35"	

Making Pink and Black Irish Chain Blocks

1. Transfer the markings for the Butterfly pattern on page 65 onto two black squares and use a backstitch to hand embroider the design with two or three strands of pink embroidery floss. Repeat for the Double Wreath pattern on page 65 with the remaining two black squares.

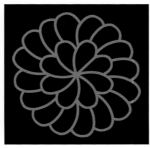

2. Sew three black 2" x 32" strips and two pink 2" x 32" strips, alternating colors beginning and ending with the black strips. Press the seam allowances toward the black fabric. Cut these strip-sets into 2" Irish Chain units. Make 15 units.

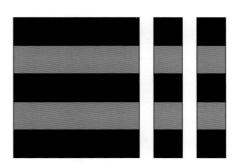

3. In the same manner, sew three pink 2" strips and two black 2" strips, alternating colors beginning and ending with the pink strips.

Press the seam allowances toward the black fabric. Cut these strip-sets into 2" Irish Chain units. Make 10 units

4. Arrange five Irish Chain units. Make five blocks.

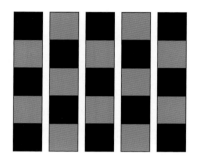

5. Stitch a black 2" x 5" strip to the top and bottom of each of the Double Wreath blocks and Butterfly blocks. Press the seam allowances away from the embroidered squares.

6. Sew a pink 2" square to the end of each of the remaining eight black strips. Press the seam allowances toward the black fabric. Stitch one of these units to each side of the embroidered blocks.

7. Sew together the four embroidered blocks with the five Irish Chain blocks according to the PINK AND BLACK IRISH CHAIN quilt assembly diagram on page 64.

Finishing Your Quilt

1. For the border, measure the quilt top from side to side through the center. Cut two strips to that length and sew these to the top and bottom of the quilt top. Press the seam allowances toward the border.

2. Measure the quilt from top to bottom through the center. Cut the remaining two border strips to that length and sew one to each side of the quilt top. Press the seam allowances toward the border.

3. Layer the quilt top, batting, and backing. Then baste the layers together and quilt as desired.

4. Sew your binding strips together end-to-end. Fold the binding strip in half lengthwise, wrong sides together, and press the fold line.

5. Place the raw edges of binding against the raw edges on top of the quilt. Sew with a ¼" seam allowance. Turn the folded edge to the back and stitch it in place.

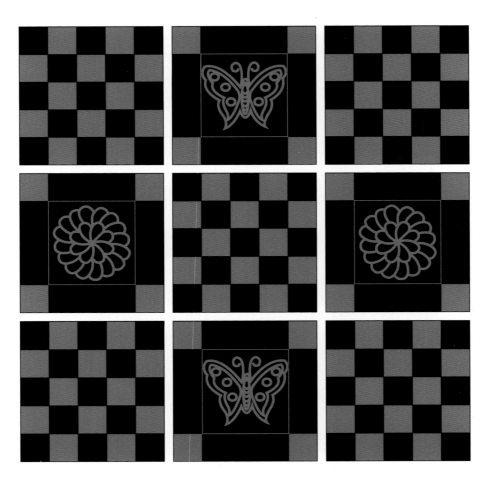

PINK AND BLACK IRISH CHAIN Quilt Assembly

**Butterfly
Embroidery Pattern**

**Double Wreath
Embroidery Pattern**

DIAMOND BAR, 66" x 66", designed and made by Sue Gilroy, Lawrenceville, Georgia.

Diamond Bar

Quilt size 66" x 66"
Block size 6" x 6"

When she designed this quilt on her computer, Susi combined a Nine-Patch block with a Rail Fence for her quilt design. She added a touch of red in the border to add sparkle to her black-and-white color scheme. Strip piecing makes this intricate design quick and easy to make.

Bold, Black & Beautiful Quilts ■ ■ ■ *Debby Kratovil*

Materials and Cutting Guide

Use fabrics at least 42" wide. All strips are cut across the width unless stated otherwise.

Materials	First Cut	Second Cut
white print, 2 yd	13 strips 2½" x 42" for blocks (strip piece)	
	10 strips 2½" x 42" for white-black-white border	
	1 strip 3⅞" x 42"	8 squares 3⅞" cut once diagonally
black print, 2½ yd	14 strips 2½" x 42" for blocks (strip piece)	
	1 strip 9¾ x 42" for side setting triangles	4 squares 9¾" for setting triangles
	1 strip 5⅛" for corner setting triangles	2 squares 5⅛" for corner triangles
	5 strips 1½" x 42" for inner border	
	5 strips 2½" x 42" for white-black-white border	
	1 strip 4¾" for cornerstones	4 squares 4¾"
red, ⅜ yd	5 strips 1½" x 42" for red border	
black solid, ⅝ yd	6 strips 2" x 42" for binding	
black-and-white stripe, ⅞ yd	7 strips 3½" for outer border	
backing, 4¼ yd	72" x 72" (pieced)	
batting	72" x 72"	

Making Nine-Patch and Rail Fence Blocks

1. Sew a 2½" white print strip between two 2½" black print strips. Press the seam allowances toward the black fabric. Make a total of five black-white-black strip-sets.

2. Cut 25 2½" units from the strip-sets for the Nine-Patch blocks.

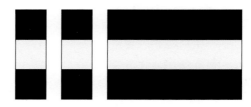

3. Sew a 2½" black print strip between two 2½" white print strips. Press the seam allowances toward the black fabric. Make four white-black-white strip-sets.

4. Cut 50 2½" white-black-white units from the strips-sets for the Nine-Patch blocks. Reserve the remaining strip-set for the white-black-white border.

5. Sew alternating units into Nine-Patch blocks, beginning and ending with white-black-white units. Make 25 blocks.

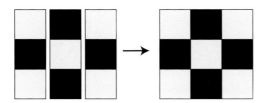

6. Cut the remaining black-white-black strip-sets into 6½" units for the Rail Fence blocks. Make 16 blocks.

Quilt Assembly

1. Arrange the blocks and setting triangles in diagonal rows, according to the DIAMOND BAR quilt assembly diagram on page 69.

2. Join the pieces together in diagonal rows. Then sew the rows together.

Adding Borders

(Piece border strips as needed to make the following borders.)

1. For the inner black print border, measure the quilt from side to side through the center. Make two 1½" strips that length and sew these to the top and bottom of the quilt. Press the seam allowances toward the border.

2. Measure the quilt from top to bottom through the center. Make the remaining two black 1½" strips that length and sew these to the sides of the quilt. Press the seam allowances toward border. This dark inner border will make your blocks look like they are floating.

3. Repeat steps 1 and 2 to add the red 1½" border

4. Measure the quilt for the white-black-white border and make four strip-sets the appropriate length. Sew two of these to the sides of the quilt.

5. To make the diamond corner blocks, finger press one 4¾" black print square in half in both directions to mark the center of each side. Finger press your white print corner triangles (cut from 3⅞" squares) on the long side to find the center.

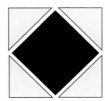

6. Matching the finger-pressed centers of the square and the triangle, sew one triangle to each side of the square. Make four corner blocks.

7. Sew a corner block to each end of the remaining two strip-set borders. Then sew these to the top and bottom of the quilt top.

8. Add the striped border to the quilt as you did for the black print and red borders.

Finishing Your Quilt

1. Layer the quilt top, batting, and backing. Then baste the layers together and quilt as desired.

2. Sew the binding strips together end-to-end. Fold the binding strip in half lengthwise, wrong sides together, and press the fold line.

3. Place the raw edges of binding against the raw edges on top of the quilt. Sew with a ¼" seam allowance. Turn folded edge to back and stitch it in place.

DIAMOND BAR Quilt Assembly

Colossal Chrysanthemums

Quilt size 40" x 40"
Block size 10" x 10"

Who says the center of a Dresden Plate block has to be a circle? I replaced the traditional circles with triangles in the corners – very quick indeed! Setting the blades against a bold black background added drama to this quilt and took it from ordinary to extraordinary.

Materials and Cutting Guide

Use fabrics at least 42" wide. All strips are cut across the width unless stated otherwise.

Materials	First Cut	Second Cut
template material	1 template from Chrysanthemum pattern on page 73	
black, 1⅞ yd	6 strips 42" x 10½"	16 squares 10½" for block backgrounds
8 bright prints, ¼ yd each	7 wedges each from template for flower petals	2 squares each 3" for flower centers
bright print, ⅜ yd	4 strips 2" x 42" for binding	
backing, 1½ yd	44" x 44" (pieced)	
batting	44" x 44"	

Making Chrysanthemum Blocks

1. Fold a wedge in half lengthwise, right sides together and stitch ¼" along the end as shown in (a). Clip away a tiny triangle of fabric to reduce bulk (b). Fold out to the right side and press, taking care to center the seam (c). Using a different color for each one, make five blades.

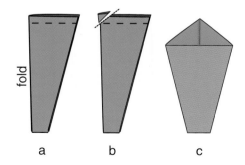

2. Stitch together five blades into a simple fan shape. Press seams flat and appliqué to a 10½" black square, aligning the raw edges of

the outside blades with the raw edges of the black square.

3. Draw a diagonal line on the wrong side of one 3" bright print square. Place the square right side down on the corner of the black square, aligning the raw edges of the two squares and taking care that the drawn diagonal line runs the same way as shown.

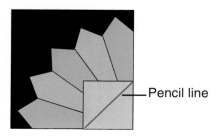

Pencil line

4. Sew along the drawn line and trim the excess from both squares (a). Press the triangle open for a completed Chrysanthemum block (b). Make 12 blocks.

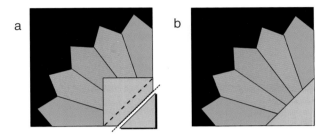

5. With the addition of the four remaining 10½" black squares, sew four rows of four blocks each according to the COLOSSAL CHRYSANTHEMUMS quilt assembly diagram below.

Finishing Your Quilt

1. Layer the quilt top, batting, and backing. Then baste the layers together and quilt as desired.

2. Sew your binding strips together end-to-end. Fold the binding strip in half lengthwise, wrong sides together, and press the fold line.

3. Place the raw edges of the binding against the raw edges on top of the quilt. Sew with a ¼" seam allowance. Turn the folded edge to the back and stitch it in place.

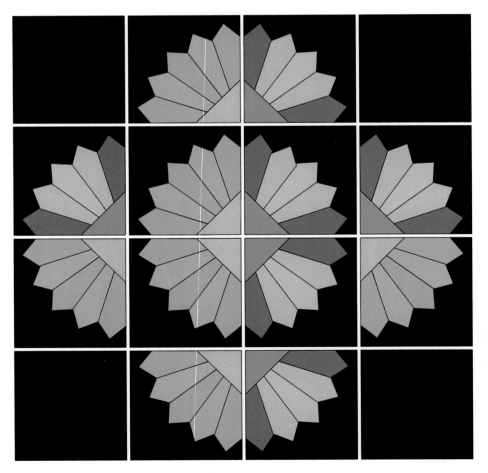

COLOSSAL CHRYSANTHEMUMS Quilt Assembly

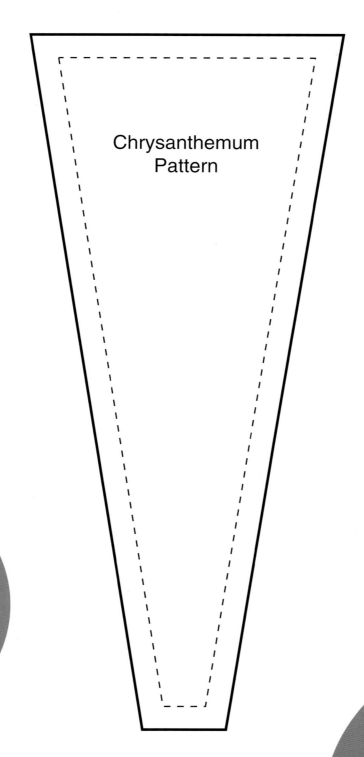

Chrysanthemum
Pattern

SWEET SLICE OF SUMMER, 37½" x 37½.", made by Diane Leighton, Yuba City, California

Sweet Slice of Summer

A twist on Log Cabin piecing and a simple appliqué Drunkard's Path block make this delicious quilt conjure up thoughts of juicy, sweet slices of fruit shared with friends at a backyard summer picnic. With just the right fabrics, summer can be savored year round with this quilt.

Quilt size: 37½" x 37½"
Block size 6" x 6"

Materials and Cutting Guide

Use fabrics at least 42" wide. All strips are cut across the width of the fabric unless stated otherwise.

Originally, I made this quilt with watermelon novelty prints. The fabrics described in this guide and in the sewing instructions coincide with the quilt pictured on page 74. You can substitute other novelty prints for the watermelon prints. Let your imagination and a trip to your local fabric store guide you in creating your own juicy blocks.

Fabric	First Cut	Second Cut
template material	1 template from the Slices pattern on page 78	
lightweight interfacing	2 squares 6½"	
black solid, ⅝ yd	1 strip 6⅞" x 42"	5 squares 6⅞" for blocks and outer watermelon setting
	1 strip 5⅛" x 42"	3 squares 5⅛" and 1 square 3⅛" for outer watermelon setting
	4 strips 2" x 42" for binding	
red with black seeds, ¼ yd	1 strip 6¼" x 42"	2 squares 6¼" for outer watermelons and 5 squares 3⅞" for inner watermelons
white multi-print, ¼ yd	4 strips 1" x 42"	18 strips 1" x 7" for rinds
green and black stripe, ⅜ yd	5 strips 1½" x 42"	18 strips 1½" x 8½" for inner watermelons
tone-on-tone or solid green, 1 fat eighth	2 squares 7¼" for outer watermelons	
deep pink, ⅜ yd	5 strips 1½" x 42" for inner and outer sashing	6 strips 1½" x 6½" 4 strips 1½" x 20½" 2 strips 1½" x 22½"
black-and-white small check, ¼ yd	4 strips 1½" x 42" for middle sashing	
watermelon print, ⅝ yd	4 strips 4½" x 42" for border	
backing, 1¼ yd	40" x 40"	
batting	40" x 40"	

Making a Log Cabin Sweet Slices Block

1. Cut one red print 3⅞" square in half along the diagonal.

2. Sew two white multi-print 1" strips to the two short sides, using a Log Cabin piecing method. Trim the edges at an angle even with the red triangle.

3. Add two black-and-green striped 1½" strips in the same way. Trim the edges at an angle as before.

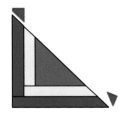

4. Cut one black 6⅞" square in half on the diagonal. Sew one black triangle to the watermelon triangle. Make nine blocks. (Reserve leftover black triangle for outer watermelon setting.)

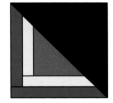

5. Sew one horizontal row with three watermelon blocks to two 6½" pink sashing strips, beginning and ending with a watermelon block. Make three rows.

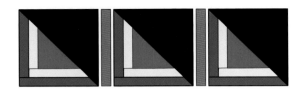

6. Join the three rows with four 20½" sashing strips, beginning and ending with a sashing strip according to the SWEET SLICE OF SUMMER quilt assembly diagram on page 77. Then add one 22½" sashing strip to each side.

7. Add the black-and-white checkered sashing strips to the sides, then the top and bottom of the quilt center. Press toward the checkered sashing.

Making Drunkard's Path Watermelon Slices

Here is a quick way to appliquéd quarter circles without using freezer paper:

1. Trace (but don't cut) the Slices template onto the wrong side of one red seed 6¼" square. The tracing is your sewing line.

2. Place a piece of lightweight interfacing under the square (against the right side of the fabric) and sew all around the drawn circle (a). Trim edges to within ⅛" of the sewn line. Clip into the interfacing (b) and turn the circle right side out and press. The raw edge of the circle is now neatly turned under, ready to be appliquéd. Make two units.

3. Center the circle on top of one green 7¼" square. Use white thread and a decorative stitch to appliqué the circle in place, then press flat.

a b

4. Turn the green square over and trim away fabric and interfacing from underneath the circle. Press again. Make two units.

5. Cut the units twice on the diagonal, yielding four triangles. Cut both units to make eight slices in all.

6. Sew the slices and black setting triangles according to the SWEET SLICE OF SUMMER quilt diagram below.

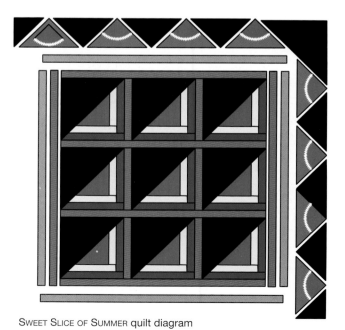

SWEET SLICE OF SUMMER quilt diagram

Finishing Your Quilt

1. For the pink inner border, measure the quilt from side to side through the center. Cut two inner-border strips to that length and sew these to the quilt top and bottom. Press the seam allowances toward the border.

2. Measure the quilt from top to bottom through the center. Cut the remaining two inner-border strips to that length and sew one to each side of the quilt. Press the seam allowances toward the border.

3. Repeat steps 1 and 2 to add the outer border. Press the seam allowances toward the border.

4. Layer the quilt top, batting, and backing. Then baste the layers together and quilt as desired.

5. Sew your binding strips together end-to-end. Fold the binding strip in half lengthwise and press the fold line.

6. Place raw edges of binding against raw edges on top of the quilt. Sew with a ¼" seam allowance. Turn the folded edge to the back and stitch in place.

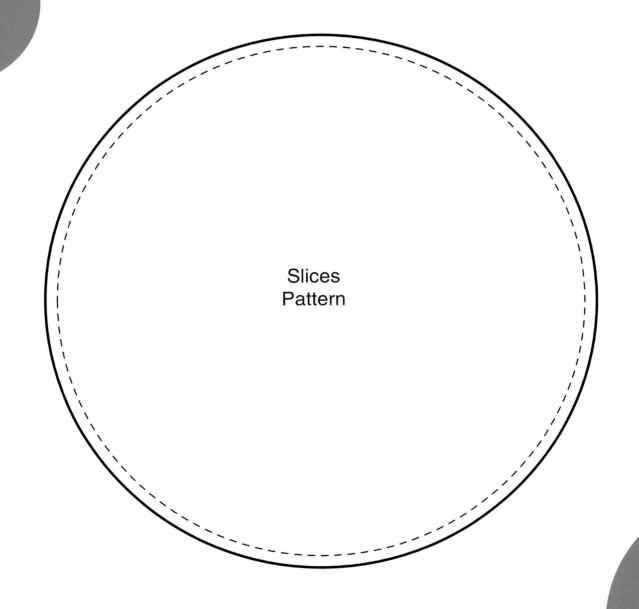

Slices
Pattern

About the Author

Debby Kratovil is a quilting teacher and prolific writer. She has been special projects editor for *Quilt Magazine* for ten years and says she enjoys teaching through the written word. Debby shares her patterns and techniques on her Web site, www.quilterbydesign.com, one of the oldest quilting sites on the Internet.

Debby has been dubbed the "power quilter" by her friends for the sheer number of quilts she makes. Always motivated by the challenge of a new design and its execution in fabric, she creates traditional quilts with a contemporary flair.

Debby is active with her quilt guild, The Material Girls of Tucker, Georgia. She and her husband, Phil, live in Atlanta; they have three daughters and a son-in-law.

Other AQS Books

This is only a small selection of the books available from the American Quilter's Society. AQS books are known worldwide for timely topics, clear writing, beautiful color photos, and accurate illustrations and patterns. The following books are available from your local bookseller, quilt shop, or public library.

#5850   us$21.95

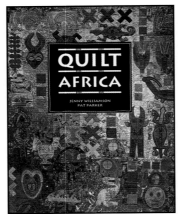

#6510   us$21.95

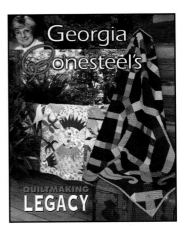

#6415   us$29.95

#6296   us$25.95

#6076   us$21.95

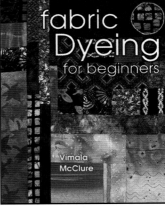

#6206   us$19.95

#6419   us$24.95

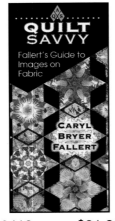

#6413   us$21.95

#6509   us$22.95